ABOUT THE AU

James Graham was born in Ayrshire in 1939. His work has been published by Edinburgh University Press, the Glasgow Centre for the Contemporary Arts, the Ragged Raven Press, *Poetry Scotland*, *Markings*, *Stonexus* (the journal of the American Stone Foundation), and others. He is especially happy to have had several poems published in *The Dark Horse*, the international poetry review edited by Gerry Cambridge. His poems have also appeared widely on the internet, most notably in the poetry journal *Three Candles*. He is currently a 'site expert' and tutor in verse-writing with the internet writers' community Write Words (writewords.org.uk).

This is his second collection. His first, *When Certain Fruits were Ripe*, was published in 2000 by the National Poetry Foundation.

JAMES GRAHAM

Clairvoyance

Selected Poems 1990-2007

Matador
9 De Montfort Mews
Leicester LE1 7FW, UK
Tel: (+44) 116 255 9311 / 9312
Email: books@troubador.co.uk
Web: www.troubador.co.uk/matador

ISBN 978-1906221-089

Typeset in 12pt StempelRoman Garamond by Troubador Publishing Ltd, Leicester, UK

Matador is an imprint of Troubador Publishing Ltd

For Jean

CONTENTS

AUTHOR'S NOTE

One day when I was about five years old I saw a soldier with a rifle running bent double through a neighbour's garden, and disappearing into the woods. There were bell-tents nearby, and I knew he wasn't an enemy but he was something of an apparition nevertheless. Born into a world at war, I was lucky to be safe from it; during the bombardment of the shipyards we heard only its distant punctuations. We lived with oil lamps, wet batteries and other archaic props. There were buses on the main road, but my father still hitched his master's horse to a gig and drove to the smithy.

I was lucky too to have been young, not in the age of the Black Death or the Inquisition, but during the brief twentieth-century heyday of the social-democratic consensus, when all our politicians thought it worthwhile to provide free health care and education. So my father was a country labourer, and I was able to attend Glasgow University and earn a degree in English Literature and Language.

And for thirty-three years I taught Shakespeare, Burns and the apostrophe – this last entirely in vain – and meanwhile entered an age of travel. I never reached the ends of the earth, but brought home a piece of quartz from the shore of Lake Huron and a picture of myself standing respectfully before the statue of Marx and Engels in Berlin. The cities of Berlin and Cordoba are especially precious to me, as well as the nearby, neighbourly city of Glasgow. And there is at least one place far from cities: the mainland of Orkney, where at the standing stones of Brodgar I made my longest journey across time, far greater than the span between oil lamps and the internet.

I wish to thank Johnathon Clifford of the National Poetry Foundation for his brusque and practical advice during the preparation of my first collection in 1999-2000. I learned a good deal from him about what works and what doesn't. I am grateful to my friends in the internet writers' community Write Words, for their constructive criticism and warm support. And to my wife Jean, for perceptive criticism and affirmation in equal measure, and for helping me believe in the merit of these poems.

Kirbuster Farm, Orkney

Peat-incense drifts towards the roof-vent,
much of it lingering, milder than acrid
coal-smoke, sweeter even than wood.

Like the stoic love
of the last family here, this fire
is at the centre of the room,
founded against a grand old stone.

Peat lies to hand in the neuk.
A settle and an Orkney chair tall-backed
and deeply curved like a half-barrel
drew children, wife and husband
into the sooty circle of love.

Soft flesh beneath this carapace,
far safer than any ancient turtle,
slept in a bed of three stone sides and roof
wrought from the very cliffs of Yesnaby.

Gales sigh against these walls.
'I'll huff and I'll puff',
sighs the dog-tired wind.

The boot of God
could stamp on this and it would stand.

Clairvoyance

There's darkness at both ends of time.

I'd like the scrying-glass to turn away
from the nothingness of futures, and reveal

a cave perhaps, smoke-black and flickering,
the first snow whirling in its mouth, the last
arrivals stumbling in. I'd like to see
the maskers' fearful and familiar dance.

I'd like to know what made this ecstasy,
what leaf or root or language fed its fire;
out of what sky the first awakenings,
out of what earth the recognitions came.

Today the western mountains, thinly snowed,
hang in the air above a fallen cloud,
silent, arcane, remote as Thule.

Show me the earth compacting from a cloud,
and how it cooled and crusted, and the lichens came,
and then the grasses and the brush, the bellowing
animals, and the talking ones; but show me those

especially who made the prophecy.

Stone Circle

The most I've ever done is sense a ghost: not see,
but sense. No more perhaps than think it possible.

The people are all here. My embassy to them
is overtaxed; my best interpreter is at a loss
to excavate away the midden of time, the plastic

language of money and explosives. We need to get
a lot of tinpots on the skip before we talk, discard
celebrity, employment, entertainment, leisure,

down through the strata to these ghosts.
But then – if my interpreter were minded to flesh out,
or cherry-pick, talk up a little what he manages to hear -

I'd like to hear him say there was no power,
no beaded idle chieftain in the Maeshowe tomb,
but the finest quarryman only buried there,

the honoured handaxe-maker and the bard,
they only, buried there when their bones were clean,
and after ceremony within this circle.

It is August now in my time and language,
when the leaves on the ghosts of ancient trees
begin to yellow, and the grain is ready

to be sweated from its chaffy stubbornness
into winter food. This season, there is plenty.
These folk to whom I cannot speak, my devious

ambassador informs me, will gather here again,
playing on bird-bones, dancing for the harvest;
and in the season for betrothals, when young men

and girls from all the islands, and the great southern land,
will come to choose and to be chosen. Did you, I ask
in my patois overgrown with history, bring these great stones

from Yesnaby cliffs, and stand them upright here,
as servants of a master? For ourselves, I am told, no less
than for our king: to acknowledge the Sun, receive

its messages, to let it speak in the darkest part
of the tomb at the Winter solstice; and most of all
to honour all the dead whose blood is in us.

I fancy I make out a word, a phrase.
Time clears like a sea-mist. I translate.

Stone

I brought a stone from the river,
from just below the humpback bridge,
where I once possessed a little cave
under the bare roots of a beech.

Sleek stones, familiar as furniture.
I called them treasure-markers then.

Now they are nameless,
stranger than moon-rocks.

Something lies heavy in my rockery
among stars of something I call saxifrage.

You'd think, if not sight,
then touch would prove it,

but even if you made it sweat,
could squeeze it like a sponge
until your fingers met, even then
you would fail to know it.

The word assigned it by the water
is not disclosed by its unforthcoming heart,
nor by the flood that silted its rough hide.

In the spate of what we call time's river,
meaning loses touch with stone.

On long school afternoons I'd drift away
from rocky-mountain geography, reach out
left-handed for the steadying beech-root,
lodge in the temple of the stone.

I weigh it here and now, and lay it down.
I've not brought home the meaning of the stone.

Creatures of the Burgess Shale

The little delicate corpses
of the creatures of the Burgess Shale
they have exhumed, and named.

Wiwaxia corrugata, tiny
spiny nut, diminutive dodo
of the ocean sediment;

Dinomischus isolatus,
solitary crocus, animal-flower;

and dream-inducing, rare
Hallucigenia sparsa:

numerous once, perhaps
even for an epoch. Pioneers
of failure to adapt, they couldn't know
how beautiful they were, or see
the world would have no use for them.

How soon the extinction
of the beautiful misfits

– the knowing animals too, the lost
Neanderthals, Tasmanians, Indians,
those who made room for strangers:

mouse-people, once self-named, then later
falsely named – they too must be unearthed.

Mouse-people born for the hawk, they
would have known that they were beautiful.

At an Iron-Age Fort

Hear it beneath our feet, an after-sound
of Kakadu and Altamira, con sordino, waiting.

Noon-bell of Jerusalem, not synchronous
with the running days and nights of fiery towns.
Noon-bell of Jerusalem, indifferent
to the moor-grass tides the loud wind makes.

Their molecules survive. It is their woven cloth
we have, their pottery and blades. It is their long
conspiracy against the predator, and their eventual
husbandry. It is their seasons of epiphany:
bands meeting bands when certain fruits were ripe,
eyes meeting eyes, at troubled leisure to invent
the ambiguity of stones, the fearful irony of bones,
the temperament and dominance of the sun.

Surfaces change: new adzes and new forms of fire
are heard of every day. We live vivace and veloce,
and animals rare and far away, and foreign seas,
and carnivals under many suns, and painted folk,
are seen like travellers' moments in a train;
through hell-for-leather wars and terrors, fashionable gods,
and wrack-and-ruin revolutions, history runs like fire;

but fathoms down the deep ground prophesies:
not soon the noon-bell and the patient festival, not soon
all things transfigured as in ancient times, not soon
the wakefulness of summer meeting-grounds.

Excursions of Mr James

Midmorning on the High Street. There he goes,
down the sunny side and past the Flower Den
and Carol's Hair Design. *There is a burial today
with flowers and necklaces.* Rough geometry

of the crusty streets, a red van turning right;
heads, shoulders, legs wagging to and fro;
Mr James there, veering to the shady side,

letting the cars and double-parked supply vans
lend him some letters to make words:
R-AEG makes aRchAEoloGy, N-RMD makes
uNReMembereD. There he goes, foreshortened,
slightly unsteady on his feet. He has heard

the women keening at the grave, and has got
his bread and apple-cakes. And everywhere
such fearful transits of the mind;
and everywhere such private lives.

He cannot seem to tell, in the moment,
whether they are women of the Susiana
or of some implacable state. He pauses
at the crossing-signal, waiting to bear

their grief to the other side. *One day
when we were skin and bone and rain,
and the glowering males dismembered*

the still, warm animal, did awareness
fire like a stricken thorn-tree and make mad
some poor strange child? And there
he hesitates and goes. *One who, already,*

could turn around in time, and see himself
from very far and high? A white car trips
on a mini-roundabout; and farther off,
the last houses and the pastureland,
the distant moving major road, the sea,
the white waves at the coast of Labrador.

Mind and Body

It used to be a baker's; and then what?
Health foods and meditation? My curiosity
too idle, and the parking spaces taken,
I never bothered to find out. Today,
it's out of business. Strange

that a thing so merely in a corner of the eye,
no former marriage-house or place of meeting
– even once only – some remembered face,
should summon such a crowd;

but even before the lights they were
unquestionably there: Altair, Jerusalem,
Sirius, Dresden, Vega, Troy

(and other lots in time and space,
none less remarkable than another):

the ancient starlight of lost multitudes, broadcast signals
from the Roman wheelwright, or the shipwright of Piraeus:
patient, expectant messages that having travelled through
both clear and cloudy ages, are now received at last, again,
uncomprehendingly, here in the studios of this anarchic city;
received much later than the signaller intended, who long ago

flamed out in pain, or whose light spirit,
collapsing into heavy bones, went out.

Anarchic skull-bound city,
its stores and workshops crowded high
in airless density, its hinterlands
unmapped and sinister,

that grows so quickly thronged
with transient poor, and purposeful
with communistic dreams: after its day

– the last call-signal started on its way,
the briefest, without the unsortable junk,
the casual mysteries of windblown paper,
street-faces and abandoned shops -

after its day, no record but the fading
word, the mouldering bones. Well,
as it happens, this is where

the winking hearse will pass, smartly towards
the boneyard on the right. And Mind and Body
will be something else by then.

Migrants

Theirs was a world of oceans
and of blue and copper trees, of cultivated
analgesic ferns, and wind and tidal power,
and many kinds of commune; their music

many-voiced, chromatic, high and deep;
their festivals passionate, masked, inspired
with aromatic smoke. But now, alas,
through alteration of the fiery universe,
their history ended and their planet

burned to ash, the last of them
drift in their ark through the profoundest
cold of space. They send their ravens
into the dark. Should they chance

upon this gemstone Earth, and find
with their petition some gargantuan dish
that hears the faint continuous

cosmic song: shall we wish them waste,
or gold-green forest, ocean, harmony?

The First Day

It was our usual path. Tom ran ahead.
Of anything uncommon, altered, I
was unaware at first; we might see, perhaps,
a squirrel or a fox, or briefly pause
in a deer's still presence. How could we know
that in one windless night without a moon
the gentle animals had gone? Instead,
a varicoloured bark, a shower of leaves,
elusive, troubling, duskily aware.

Then suddenly, a serpent on a bough,
an armoured basilisk with turning eye.
Tom would not cry, but gripped my coat.

The wiry little snakes, the natterjacks,
the crowd of geckos gave us leave, but each
stopped once at least, to make a little sting.
We ran, and did not look behind; I seemed
to hear a hunger, following not far off.
I closed the outward gate, like a story-book.

The misted morning fields we passed again;
and passed the same seven trees before the road
inclined toward the town. And all the way

Tom worried at the wonders he had seen,
and I replied with comforts. Even my own
unease began, chameleon-like, to turn

to unbelief – except that people seemed
to hurry and to turn aside, and groups

dispersed, and at their windows, faces
feared this first day and its ensuing night,
the guttering light and the disordered stars

and Tom grew still, as a child should never be;
and in the Square men smiled and smiled
and came and went, in long dark-windowed cars.

Old Snow

Long before light he wakes
and crosses the chill slate floor.

He opens the door to the snow; a little
cataract falls and shatters.

This snow, the same since ages
of the wild ox and mammoth, is the first

deep snow that will inspire him.
He leaps, and cannot see its surface;

with all the levers of his body leaps again.
He touches, sifts and shivers – and now runs

through the moon-pale house to the big bed,
and tumbles into the middle space.

The seed from which he grew
contained the joy of snow.

Discoveries

Tom found a blackbird in the grass,
and brought it home in his upturned palm
as if it were a bubble; laid it in a box, attacked

the rose-bed with a trowel and bare hands until he got three
worms; yanked one out like elastic;
offered one, which the young bird, shivering,

made slither over; collared the sidling cat
and shut her in the kitchen; found his mummy,
asked her what to do. *We found*

some bodies in the woods, a man, his face
was in the nettles, and his arm all twisted under him; a lady,
with one shoe; a boy, a big fat boy,
his eyes were kind of open.

They was all blood, all over, mostly on their heads.
We didn't run away, we looked at them,
we were like wow. What joy some day to find

beneath the ice of Titan, or the famished Martian rock,
the hairline we have laboured for, the green,
the not-quite-dead. We'll cherish that, and wish.

Elegy

I have just now observed the winter shore
in the late light whose nameless radiant grey
makes the low cliff and its farmhouse shine;
but the vast water, tame and still today,

seemed to say farewell. And I dreamed I saw
the earth from space: the lovely planet, dressed
in water and invisible oxygen
and therefore by departing voyagers blessed.

No broad-winged dragons climbed the air;
the sky was not bloody, the wind not wild.
It was not the country where griffins prey
on the innocent lamb and the innocent child.

Since then I have hastily closed my door, unfree
of the darkening shore and the death-quiet sea.

Not Knowing the Time

And first I put a little air in the tyres,
and almost without thought took off my watch.
And then the October air, and the joy of balance.

And a nod to a person I knew, who was going somewhere,
and a word to a person I knew, who carried a paper
and looked at his watch, and walked at the green man's bidding.

I rested the bike on a verge, and lay in the shade,
in the midst of the grass, the dusty delicate heads,
a long time looking upwards and lying still.

A long time looking upwards and lying still.
The airy foliage, the dry October leaves,
trembled and spun against a moving sky.

And then I turned over, to see the world under the grass:
the empty spiderways, the tortuous streets and plazas.
A solitary motion there, the last of the summer crowd.

A long time lying still and living in the grass,
like a mouse or deer on the sea-floor, or bright
fish drifting and steering among the crowns.

Night Thought

We learn to be at home
In the world we know.

Schooled in the sea, we would be sure
that ocean names the creatures of dry earth,
and hauls the flesh of valleys in.

We'd wonder at the dryness of the rain,
and how the walking monsters live,
and eagles in the thin, bright air.

Or if the mist were sulphurous
and trees of hollow steel and copper
spat and crackled through the night,

we would believe them too, and find
the silent day-flowers strange.

Christmas Night

As daylight falls away, a wind is rising.
The garden trees begin to brace themselves
against this coming and all future storms.

But there is suddenly a paper-shower:
a pair of robins and their holly-branch
lodge in the cypress, and arcadian snow

eddies and falls upon a coaching inn
and round the bottle-glass of cottages
and in the crotch of the bending apple-tree.

The dark is full of emblems of the sun.
Soon paper Christmas trees will fall like leaves
and aureoled wandering candles not go out,

and wishful kings and shepherds come and go,
and the robins rise again, and the snow depart.
This rattling night will wreck the calendar,

warping and snapping the connected hours.
Visions will pass the window as I sleep,
but I will wake, and know what day it is,

and gather up the ages of the world,
set times and turning-points upon their feet,
lose like a dream the courage to be lost.

New Year's Eve

Clocks chime midwinter, giving notice
among fresh kisses and the shaking
of forgotten hands, that death and malice
of the frost surrender to the making
of green treaties by lapsed friends.

The year's senility ends.
Among this company, exchange of giving
drink, fuel and love, suspends
the need for judgment except judging
to be good. Its meaning lies

boundless about us, like the galaxies,
yet human here beside the encircled hearth.
Our handshakes are all drunken ecstasies,
but true for all that, truer than virgin birth.

Day's Work

After weeks of rain, I heave and shove the mower
through the heavy grass, and hunkering gouge
the damp green gobbets from its moving parts.
I clear a circle round the birch, and plunge
my hands into a fine composted bark
and lay and smooth it round the stem.
I hoe some weeds and let them dry in the sun.

My neighbour has a clock that chimes
on every hour, but doesn't count the hours.
This is play-labour, neither waged nor feudal.
And you might come and look, and I might point
to where the mown grass seems to smoulder
among the wavering shadows of the tree,
and then it would be yours as well as mine.

Careful to save the soil, I rake the weeds
and mound and shovel, bag and barrow.
Remembering a wound the chafing wind
has gouged in an alder-stem against its stake,
I unfetter the good tree, and clean the stem,
and dress it with healing stuff, to make it safe.

Blackbird

Every day, if I disturb
the soil at all, he follows me
and gleans. He swallows
everything that moves.

I tossed him two short worms.
He didn't flinch (him, flinch?
a finch would flinch, not him)
but deftly tweezered them,

then bounded nearly up to me,
fanned and jiggled his folded wings,
and cocked a look at me
with his starboard eye.

I wonder why – when the crowd
around the peanut feeder
spring instantly at my slightest
twitch, and catapult themselves

off into trackless wilderness –
why he, this pair of cold, fresh
gift-worms writhing in his beak,
comes up to me in six or seven

little long-jumps? I know it's not
a thank-you, and I'm glad he has
no inkling of charity. I'd rather think
he is accustomed, bold, in all

his dealings with all flesh;
that, perfect connoisseur, he has
evaluated and rejected me
as being too much to swallow.

Tom-noddies

Outdoors for a moment at ten to eleven,
I am drenched by a flurry of cries, a seaspray
of gusting, combative cries. And so long as I

do not walk over and look, they are skirlies:
little auks, kittiwakes, rockdoves, tom-noddies.
So long as I do not walk over and look,

their soaring and freedom take my breath.
Over the school fence they soar in the height
and depth of their freedom, over the fence,

out over the rocks and rollers. But the wind
brings over the housetops the little bell, too,
not a sea-bell, the little peremptory bell.

Skirlies – sea-birds
Tom-noddies – puffins

Honeysuckle

This parasite has bound
the lilac limb by limb.

Rummaging and ravening and alchemising
rain and soil to scrawny timbers, it has built
its tensile structure, stretching and pushing out
deep-breathing leaves and airless heavy scent.

It has whizzed this spring across the earth,
under the harebell camouflage, begun
to scale the weeping birch, will colonise

it quickly. Such energy, it ought to whine
like some steel grid. It never tires,
will keep on growing when it's dead.

Such life! – my words are calumny; they
have made a wicked caricature, distorted this
unconscious thing that's neither beautiful

nor ugly, but alive – and can do worse:
speak of the honeysuckle-scented tyranny,
the moneysuckle reaching across oceans,

suckering and blossoming in every city,
red and blue and yellow to entice us,
the plazas filled with wishes. But whatever

it may be I happen to call honeysuckle,
and someone else calls *chèvrefeuille*
or *madreselva*: it isn't what I make of it.

My monster's a word-honeysuckle merely;
it gorges in the severed world of language.

From where I stand, the land
falls gently away, and the ocean
touches it, and touches Africa.

But something lives out there.
Something more solid than conceits
preys on the cities and the fields.

Leidseplein

It should be possible to read a place, but here
you have to read the guide-book. Here the past
has been demolished and the rubble cleared.

Here, once upon a time, all travellers from Leiden
by horse-vehicles were obliged to halt, and leave
them in this open space or 'plein'. (Ah! hence the name.)

And once upon another time, young communists
tried with their songs and hardly innocent red flags
to turn the fascist tide. But here and now -

this ahistoric now, this barely geographic here -
it's Burger King, Hitachi, Coca-Cola, Michelob;
they wink and jab you in the ribs, a parody

of greeting that you can't respond to; and you feel
the sour banality of travel, coming after many hours
to the flashy, big-beat sameness of this place.

It should be possible to hear this as a scherzo,
that jazzes up an earlier theme or two; there should
be tokens of heredity, high cheekbones, eyes; but here

you turn a page, and suddenly it's esperanto.
But this is a moment in history too, and my
being in it at a table with Big King and fries

makes it no less actual, or more complete,
than for the Dutch communists in their day.
They couldn't see an end to fascist thuggery, nor I

to the honeysuckle of consumerism, which bears
these pretty flowers. There's a time, I realise,
in the individual life when in some market-places,

at certain hours of the day, it suddenly becomes
much harder to take in what's being said, for it's
the older language only that you speak. At least

it's a peaceful crowd, whoever they may be. This is
a moment too, this too is once upon a time.

Amsterdam, May 2002

Survivor

I have lived in peace; I never saw
a terrorist's gesture mingle stone and bone.
Our streets are breezy with the call
of curry spice, and wines;

and I have earned the price,
sweating to teach, this reaching out
to heave the children of the poor
over some sheer

and treacherous rock, toward revelations
they will lose on the closing bell.
And I have issued verse
that some have praised;

and the children of my line
go free. It is the same
molecular key, the marvellous
rope we may yet learn to read,

that made the child who is cradled now
in a fireman's arms. In his hurt eyes
no ecstasy of trust; such light
as rivals May, such knowing light,

in him is dust, and he will die.
But I, extravagant, may walk
this tidy town, and no man blow
to smithereens longevity such as mine.

Running Away

At the age of eight
I ran away
from the Korean War.
On the first four notes
of Big Ben's tune
(*it's-time-to-go*)

I made for my room,
and studied my jigsaw
or read *Alice.*
My cat Doodlebug –
I wished she could grin.

I never went back
to the Korean War.

Much later, at fifty,
running away again,
this time from the *son et lumière*
in the Gulf in 1991,

buying no papers, turning aside
from the news to read *Don Quixote,*
an accidental headline
got through my defences:

THE MOST TERRIBLE ASSAULT
ON A RETREATING ARMY
IN THE HISTORY OF WARFARE

– afraid to read on,
it was two years or more
before I could look closely
at that turkey shoot, that 'killing
unequalled since Hiroshima';
the dead uncounted, despised,
bulldozed into the sand.

I'm as grown-up now
as I'll ever be, and still
sometimes on a garden afternoon
the White Rabbit hurries by.

But there's no place
where it's always six o'clock,
or where the falling soldiers
are mere sheep

and the dead
were bulldozed
into the sand.

Something Happened

A man took a knife
and cut me below the ribs.
I had a three-inch wound.
I've still got the scar.

I'm glad, though,
that before he sliced me
his mate had knocked me out
with a phial of good liquor.

In the hours that followed,
some realisations came.

I thought about things
I had never done,
and felt quite happy
never to have done them.

I have never, I realised,
used a gun. Never ever
taken potshots at rabbits
or my parents, or children
in a classroom, or men
in different coloured suits
under different command.

And then I realised
I'd never even touched a gun.

I thought at first
I must be self-deluded,
but it's true:

I never *touched* one, not even
a feather-touch with one finger
for one tenth of a second.
Old muskets in museums:
'Please do not touch'.
I never did.

Except for a toy
my mother bought me
cause I said I wanted it.

With shooter in one hand
and potato in the other,
I toted for one day,

until my pacificist father
came home from work,
gave me a quiet talk
and disarmed me for ever.

So apart from that
one single day, I've never
used or handled or touched
or been closer
than arm's length to a gun.

But in those tender hours and days
after the man so kindly cut me,
another realisation came.

I understood the meaning of a wound,
a three-inch wound below the ribs,
made with a knife

or gun.

A little wound. Not a gaping hole
in the abdomen, the small
intestines spilling out. Not

the tibia in smithereens,
a severed arm, a ruined hand.
Just a superficial wound.

When the enemy attacks
they don't send in detachments
of anaesthetists. They make
their three-inch, six-inch, nine-inch wounds

while you're awake; they set
you on fire with pain. I never
had any dealings with those
rough surgeons, but I thought

of all the young men who ever had;
who ever had even a little wound
to the soft flesh, while wide awake.

Verdict

The murder trial is meticulous:
the science of stains and tissue,
the jury solemnly advised;

so much contention, such pains
about the truth. These single deaths
are cosseted like neolithic bones. Not so

the public murders: *son et lumière*
spiced with a *frisson* of invisible death,
subtle performance art. These deaths

are of another category, the murderers
untouchable as ancient kings. They make
their fictions work for them: their gods,

their borderlines on maps, mythology of trade,
the democratic spectacle. The case
will not be heard. There is an audience

of witnesses, but the broken child
and the desolate mother are denied
even the slight honour of a scrupulous

forensic. In any case, the miscreants
were never present. Not for them the terrors
and postponements of death row; at worst,

a scandalgate, a critical biography, an academic
judgement: verdict of that history they bought
and took possession of, that special freedom.

Akademeia

1

We are always new to the world. In old age
we are still strangers; the earth's mantle

knows too much, and there's no time
to master all the disciplines: seismology of war,
astrology of power, pathology of empire.

'I dote on myself, there is that lot of me and all so luscious'
- that was Whitman on his body; at my age it's the mind
more than the body, but that will do well enough; I can spend
whole days in my head and not go out, I never get tired of it.

I do not avoid its hinterlands, its ghettos and battlefields,
its woodland paths where turning a corner I have found
a family of burned-out Slovak gipsies, living in a dugout.

Sometimes I walk down a particular steep path among gorse,
through dog-daisies and meadowsweet to the spongy riverbank
and, if the stepping-stones are high and dry, cross over to the ruins,
and enter Carthage by the one remaining gate.

I scour the windy courts and palaces, sifting and testing
for traces of the minerals that feed the bones of the poor,
memorialising the peasants without bread, the corpses
on the ice before Kronstadt, the frozen corpses of Kolyma.

I gather the spectres out of the dusty wind: zeks tired to death;
peasants eating their dogs, their dead, and the bark of trees:
hope perishing, a handful of seeds in the waterless earth.

O mia patria: my native land, so beautiful and so betrayed.

I know too little and too much, and what I know I have learned only
by casting my eye on the mediations, the historians' subjectivities,
and then through the prisms and filters of my own subjectivity,

but stranger as I am I love the people of the ruins, who made
their revolution at the worst of times. For seventy years
implacably hated, their whole western land laid waste, I mourn
their strange, deformed, retarded, wearisome new kind of polity,
and fall silent while their anthem plays. Even so,

I hurry back to the comfortable place
I see from my window: garden, woodland and moor.
No other *akademeia* is so populous:

a crowd of common folk, their faces carved by guesswork.
As you walk among them, they look down, they do not gaze
importantly into the yonder, or they seem to have just turned
their heads to listen to you. Some too whose names are known:
a figure of Neruda side by side with Wedderburn,
and Luxemburg with Mary Bryant; Bloch, Marcuse,
'gardeners of the most mysterious tree'; Bert Brecht,
his own lines carved around the pedestal:

The children to the motherly, so that they will be loved
The carriages to the good drivers, that they be driven well
And the valley to the waterers, that it may bear fruit;

all canopied with snow-gum and Cotinus Flame,
betula pendula tristis and *rosa felicité perpetue.*

And every day in season I prick out the withering flowerlets
of the scarlet and white geraniums, and add them to the compost,

and tune every day to the Nameless Channel, which for the sake
of giving it a name I call Sloth TV, after my notion of a sloth,
which at evening drowsily notes the trees, how they take
    nourishment
from the wormy sky, and feather the birded ground;
my upturned teddy-bear, my anthropomorphic sloth,
cute logo of the unremembered.

There are no celebrity appearances, or biographies
of highnesses and majesties and mediocre excellencies,
or *Police Gazette* mass-murderers, Hitler, Suharto, Kissinger;
or tales of the old cosa nostras, the monarchies and ruling classes;

but the history of the tribes living under the mountain,
the garden people, the idle, vagrant and disaffected of all time;
the smugglers, the highwaymen, the noble beggars; the poor
who lived by exchanging stolen cloth for stolen food, who rose up
against their officers, and joined the pirates;

those who would not be toothwheels, as well as those who merely
functioned and died, while the people of the mountain, in their
    power-clothes,
caused them to work, or be hanged, or be branded 'Duke of York'.

Here I have seen, to epic music, the life of Mary Bryant,
who stole a lady's purse and cloak on the highway out of Plymouth.
But King George's thief-takers were well-informed and prompt,
and the King's magistrates great extravagant punishers.
First, below decks on a stinking hulk, then off with the First Fleet.
But Mary and her husband Will the free trader, and their
    convict crew,
took charge of the governor's boat and, dipping oars in almost perfect
silence, sailed out of Sydney Harbour on a moonless night.
She is one of Sloth TV's great women of all time.
In a nearby universe there's a calendar date for her,
a summer holiday with saxophones and drums.

The memory of those born into the world and decayed into earth
without feasting on it, all those denied the life of play and
    celebration,
I turn right way up, so that their unconsummated history
becomes true history, their thieving a virtuous act,
and their preachers of jubilee our great men and women.

2

A precarious mind to live in, even for a day! Much better, surely,
to rise every morning to my CD shower companion, and
get out more: see the bright malls, the bright logos,
the street furniture and brand exhibitions, see how good
the world is. Or join the progress north and southbound,
see the abracadabras: Eddie Stobart, famous as Socrates: eastbound,
westbound, in perpetuum mobile, telling us and telling us their
   names.
Be glad to have been born in the Golden Age, with its many
soft imperatives: *Get total comfort and support, breathe
healthier bug-free air, grab all the latest gadgets, smile
with confidence.* So many orders to be disregarded.

Yet, in a sense we obey them all. Maybe we don't
rush out and buy the solid silver computer mouse, but we
start to believe the evaporation of wealth to the high ground,
where the gated villas are, is what man was born for.
Buy if you can, but what matters is belief.

And I do go out the odd time, and go down in the rickety train,
down to the centre of things; but soon come rattling back to
   my head
with its back room full of books, its screen of lilac, its hinterland.

Internal exile in the land of the subtle Santa Claus tyrants,
as if clandestinely I write about the Kader fire, in Thailand in '93:
188 young women sewing up Bugs Bunnys and yellow Bart
   Simpsons
were burned or suffocated: *the Serpent Temples thro the Earth
Resound with cries of Victims, shouts & songs & dying groans
And flames of dusky fire*: I write verse even less fettered than
   Blake's,

raging furious at the furnaces, chastising the huge obscene wealth
of the international gewgaw trade: with many tears lamenting
the young women, like creatures evolved to sustain the predators,
sleeping on the floors of the gewgaw-makers' dormitories,
in spaces marked out like car-parks. I want to cram these atrocities

into a prosy poetry, verse with a great whalebone stuck in its throat,
that chokes on neoliberal order and new paradigms of power,
and doesn't sing at all; that goes on about state murder,

not only the pity of it, but the economics and politics,
or the criminology rather, how the guilty are exempt:
Nixon for example, guilty of burglary and foul language
but scot-free on the murder of the wife and children
of the Cambodian soldier found by the roadside crying,
'They have killed them all! All my family are dead!'

3

In the early years of what is called the new millenium, rather
than pretend to go forward I often dawdle and look back,
even wander back, to the times I have grown used to;
   and whenever
I venture as far as the part of the woods where the ground gives way
and the chafing rhododendrons and creaking willows vex and rile,

I find some papers on me, a communist identity and passport;
I don't know what to do with it, it troubles me; but I remember
the men who crossed the Pyrenees and let their bones be shattered,
or died sometimes in the first minutes of battle: ghosts and veterans
of the first war against fascism, betrayed by Moscow and democracy,
but nourished by an ancient pride, born on the plains of the
   palaeolithic.

It is only in their terrain and mine, in the lands of the federation,
that the diagnostics are true and young trees not torn out by
   the roots,
but pruned and coppiced and cleansing fire sent sometimes
   through them;
here we have husbandry, confirm ourselves in work and play,
   belong
not to another but to ourselves. 'The truths of the earth
   continually wait'

but my garden has long since overflowed: the forest and the moors
are filled with terracotta men and women hanged
or broken on the wheel. It's common land, beyond the gates,
and yet I seem to be the ranger, making my journey every day;
recognising the chants and cries of the migrant dead,
keeping the moors and forest a habitat, a populous memory.

Jack Sheppard

Let us recite his deeds. His hands more versatile
than goldsmith's tools, the whole sweet mechanism
between brain and fingers exquisitely tuned, he made a jest

of locks and bolts, a fool of Rackall the drunken turnkey.
Departing the Stone Room was his greatest work.
Muscling and narrowing his craftsman's hands,

he streamlined them free of the cuffs; then worked
with a silly nail at the ankle-chains; with a link of broken chain
he rooted out the chimney-bar; with a railing-spike

he forced four doors; at last, emerging in free air but high
above the surrounding roofs, he turned, went back (went back!
such mastery of suspense!) to fetch some shinning-blankets.

Mayhew's children, without schooling, knew his name.
Master gaol-breaker, exemplar of the dangerous poor, he was
their Alexander. It was the little men

of property he robbed, from whom he gathered watches,
linen swatches, bric-à-brac; but could not forage
among Lords and Commons, they who would not 'open

bags and barns, and make the earth a common treasury'.
A hundred thousand came to see him hanged.
The Tyburn crowd: their skulls deep-mined; clear-

felled their wildwood; harried of their rubies, gold,
obsidian, diamonds; one and all they mourned their chief,
who seemed to have opened for them a heavy door.

In Newgate, he had been a peepshow (short season only!).
The embezzler Macclesfield, the kleptomaniac Lord Chancellor,
was once his audience there; the greater drew the less.

A carpenter to trade, he could masquerade
as butcher, botcher, beggar, porter – badges
of servitude he wore ironically. And once

in a carriage driving through the arch of Newgate,
he was a star, a maestro. But 'they hang poor men
if they do steal, having taken from them all their maintenance';

born in the prison-camp at Spitalfields, fettered from birth,
he could not redeem his neighbours' loss. Yet Mayhew's
children acknowledged him; even we who have walked

across the blasted plain, stood in the ruins of our cities,
who habitually turn our keys in the double locks
of our house-doors: we have not lost him yet.

Landmark

A puddled space between a store-back
and a wall. No doors or gates or windows
to make it useful, no pathetic ornament
to make it even ironically beautiful.

No passage to wherever. A poly-bag
turns over, yawns, and rests. Some
green stuff, plastic strip, in disarray.
A capsized trolley, wasteland cliché.

Such a nothing place, it's odd the walls
don't just cave into it. Still, it has
no golden god, no humble congregation.
No fugitive has made his last stand here.

A quiet, useless canyon. Name it then,
bestow the geographer's accolade:
sea-name perhaps, the Moonless Deep;
moon-name, the Sea of Rains.

No, let it be washed and gilded, given
an earth-name, one of the multitude;
let it commemorate 'a poor woman, Alice,
drowned by London Wall'; call it

the Alice Monument, let it have souvenirs
and yellow signs and guards and guides,
and let it flaunt the somethingness of waste,
the frail celebrity of the drowned.

At the Marx-Engels-Forum in Berlin

Marx sits and Engels stands. Their backs
are to the empty glasshouse of the former
unlamented GDR. They would be happy,
I surmise, to know the whispering, askance

res publica of spies is gone, and glad
to wander through the trees and down the Linden,
where Moor could pace about and stretch his legs
while Engels rested after standing fifty years.

And in this market that has taken root
beyond the Wall, they might end up in Dressler's
(Engels paying), dine on schnitzel and get drunk,
and nobody, not the waiter, not the comrade

at the corner table, could add a single word
to the old interminable book of heresies.
This city's taking long, deep breaths, unwinding
in the October sun. I have just walked down

from Prenzlauer Berg, where the chestnut trees
of Kollwitzplatz, the children's climbing frame,
the tenement façades, have slept and slept.
Among the trees, like an archetypal granny,

a bronze of Käthe Kollwitz, who began to draw
the poor, 'because I found them beautiful';
her woman with an earring, her bound peasant,
her chatting women, brothers, man and woman,

weavers, pregnant woman, are all strong
and beautiful and do not sleep. You look
them in the eye and they begin again
their advocacy that was overruled

by the gangsters of the former Reich and by
the mobsters of the former revolution.
So I return to the seated Marx and upright
Engels, and remember how they got

the diagnosis right, and the prognosis wrong,
and the shambles of a history we got
instead of health and freedom for these poor.
And I wander through the trees, and past

the Bebelplatz, where books were burned,
and down the Linden, trying to unwind.
It's only later, at the corner table, having dined
and got a little drunk, that I begin

to weep for joy, as the Party poet might have said,
to see three thousand Soviet tanks advancing
and the red flag planted on the Reichstag, and
the heroes of the revolution still not dead.

October 1998

Excursion

...and coming up now, on your left,
the famous Lovers' Rock, the *Peña
de los Enamorados*, last refuge – so
the legend has it – of a tragic pair,
young Christian man and Moorish girl
who rather than renounce their love
leapt together to their deaths

and over there, just coming into view,
the legendary Castle Chillon set against
white mountain-tops and softly lapped
by the gentle waves of Lake Geneva;
in the dungeon there, young Bonivard
was shackled to a pillar for six years
for his revolt against the Savoyards

soon after lunch we should arrive
at the Brown Bear Wildlife Park; and here's
the Taj Mahal, and there's the Parthenon;
and on your left the Alcazaba,
and on your right the Roman arch.
It's good to have the sunshine every day,
we've had some storms. And here we see

some people from some nearby villages –
quite a crowd – a few in native dress –
receiving international relief; I hear
some pulses have arrived today

as well as maize and oil. We'll take
our lunch-break at Grand Canyon Village;
then, in the afternoon, the bears...

Tribe

You arrive at the city over soaring moors.
The landmarks are white steadings, lighthouse-stark.
You seem at the edge of a different sky, and then
there is a land beyond the sky: the broad

electric meadow of the city, under the early stars,
its amber blossoms everywhere, sparse only far away
by the western ocean or the hills. I have no name
for the colours of the hills: not green,
not blue; they are the colour, I suppose,
of hillsides grassed and gorsed and marvelled at
in failing light, on this one night, a cool
rose-grey, a darkening rose. Apartment blocks
surround the college towers, like giants
that have wandered down from the romantic glens
and stand amazed. And I have seen

the water-meadows of this city too, sham tarns
that never heal, beaches for half-wild children
toying with paid-out audiotape and wrecks
and trademarked jetsam; and the apartment blocks,
cracked-windowed crates through which they squeal
with the scrawny timelessness of gulls. In the city's

scrambled heart, an old man crowned with a trampled hat
is fiercely pedalling. Beard like a mouse's nest,
he rides four lanes of motors. Presently his soft bag
quickens, and a black cat scales his dangerous shoulder,

rocking, goat-sure, tail like a pennon. I am native here

among the monuments to famous men
whose labour forces built the money-towers,
whose fighting forces have made desolation
out of cities such as this. I am aboriginal.

Glasgow, Scotland 2004

At my Mother's Grave

I've kept her clock and bible, and the specs
she wore for forty years (she used to stick
the lenses to the frames with super-glue).
From the funeral, I remember two things only:
that heads turned, and there were momentary smiles,
when Lucy said, 'It's like a box of treasure';
and the parson reading, with what seemed genuine fire,
from that awful book about the holy city.
My mother thought, or was content to think,
she'd end up there, walking the golden streets.

And now as the chopped-up turf is being healed
by rain and sun, I can't locate her. The changes
are all working now: she's rotting like a pear:
the noxious chemistry of the after-life
will render her to bones and rings. She won't
be anxious to convulse some psychic every time
I need a haircut, or to tell me to be careful.
She won't appear on some surveillance tape
or make my stairway chilly with her presence.
I wouldn't recognise her soul; she never
offered me the part of her that one
might call a soul, or wasn't able to,
or else there's no such thing. She might have kept
it in a little treasure-box. Her pride
in scarcity and economy, reiterated pride
in a table bought for less than thirty bob
a quarter-century ago: such particles

will wander in and out of non-existence
in the memory of neighbours, carers, those
who waited briefly at the grave. Whatever beads
my daughters had from her, weekends
and holidays, will be among their burial goods.

Or has she spilled into this verse like sand,
to make a crumbling post-Christian *Lycidas*?

Will a party some day find what's left of her,
and dust and scrape, and guess, and in a moment
of unscientific playfulness, rename her Lucy?

'I knew it all along', she used to say.
Back at the keyboard now, with all the playful
and evasive questions written down,
her self-defining catchphrase – not without
a certain irony in the trotting out –
becomes a whisper in my ear. Of course
I know her whereabouts. Something had left
her body long ago. Her hedgehog molecules
are in my head, and stomach too: I lack,
if not big toes, or knife-and-fork proficiency, then
people-gumption. I'm a skulker. I have the art
with which she screened humanity, her lifelong
little side-step dance – besides other mysteries
my excavations cannot solve. She haunts me
and decays in me, I am her golden city.

Elegies for my Father

1

In what sense did he own his world?
The drystone walls were written in his hand,
the tight barbed fences finished in his style.
He made a hen and chickens on the crown
of a borrowed hawthorn hedge. The estate
was an exhibition of his work.

Things, labour, horses, all belonged
to a totter-up of rents: the chestnut candles
and the dark abundant chestnut loam
and its forbidden harvest, all accounted for
to a renter of cold rooms and common stairs.

My father worked alone, in company
with sun-pools in the woods, or shivering
birch-leaves, or the early snowfall, apparitions
of his freedom, enticements to his folded self.
He seemed to hoard the place's melancholy.

2

In the midst of life, he talked of Heaven.
'In the sweet by-and-by', he softly sang
– he had no ear – to the wheezy organ.
'We shall meet on that beautiful shore'.

One day, called home from school, I heard
my mother say, 'He's gone to Heaven. He
was suffering, but now there's no more pain'.

There was more than loss, even in the first
few moments. 'Plus ça change', an older head
might have worded it, 'he'll be a handyman
to the proprietor of worlds'. Or, 'Let him steal
a barrel of this painlessness, and bring it back,
to oil our bones, and flush the cancers out'.

3

I know geraniums:
quick reddening into urgent flares,
continuous dying day by day.

My father taught me not
to hack away the still half-living heads,
but to venture thumb and finger in the fire
and carry off the little witherings only, burned
from scarlet to dry blood,

so that the tiny, ready blood-drops underneath
would be fulfilled, their guttering postponed.

Not universal death, but compost: throw
the dying on the compost, my late father said;
and sure enough in season it would mingle
with the airy soil again, and make geraniums.

My father's earth is warm; there is still
continuous dying and living there.

Annick Water

I think I came to taste
the sweet past here,
like rose-hips,
not the collapse of years.

But here's John Hastings' house,
torn beyond cure;
enduring, as stone will,
far, far too long. Through all
my childhood, he was old.
Gassed in some wasteland, cast
out coughing from the butchers' war,
he sold best suits, and gents
and ladies boots and shoes,
out of a horse-van. In the year
of the flood, rooks
racketing overhead, the rioting
Annick at his door,
his sick wife calling, he willed
the water and the wind away
and eight miles laboured
to the doctor's gate.

I see the woods have lost
the tree-house tree,
my secret neighbourhood;
– I would have mourned then
if a wind had taken it –

my neighbours too, companionable elves,
the girl with the riding hood, the wily wolf,
the bears and their fair visitor, ghosts
always, now seem grass.

I find my name here, gashed
in a ridged ash-bark.

Easy nostalgia, like a comfortable
breeze, I really
wished for, not these
edged gusts, remembrance-
bearing, as it were December.

At the Laurel Inn, Robin Hood's Bay

It was closed.
At lunch-time on a Tuesday,
it was closed.

From 1917 till 1926
my grandmother lived
in the flat above this pub.

She had lost two husbands,
both called James.

The first of the Jameses
was killed in South Africa
by rotten army food.

James the Second
died on the lip of a trench
and left three children.

She never lived to know it
but James, her only son,
was bombed in Coventry.

Still, here I was,
old James the Fourth,
the lucky one,
the post-war one,

and I wanted to drink to her
but the pub was closed.

Terrible, Terrible

The car won't start; I settle for the polar
trail, mean snow beginning as I go,
tirling and whirling in a freezing wind.

Scribbles and scratches frost the shelter's perspex.
Bent arrows pierce a triple-life-size heart.
*Rab loves...*the fancied name is frosted out.

A grey-haired tubby lady, booted, hatted,
insulated like a bear, says brightly,
'Oh! Is this no terrible? What a day!'

Unable to embark beyond weather-talk,
I'm glad to see her friend. I don't pick up
much more except a few more terribles,
and 'Aye, he's walkin' wi' twa sticks' – the joy
of lamentation, in the thickening snow.

Chronos

The daily men and women in the street
who all the way to death seem satisfied
with clocks, and queues, and the exchange
of common facts: what confidential news,
what secret promise do they have?

But the woman who in childhood played
among asbestos dust; the man
who as a boy was warned to keep
the secret of the book-store, and became
afraid to touch: their lives are single
meagre tales. For them the dust is law:

and it is so for those of us who hate
mortality because we are mocked
by summers never twice the same,
or the infinity of art, or love: we have
the news already, it is all we have.

Woman at a Bus Stop

On an uncertain day
in a dry September, my passing eye
is taken with her speckled shirt
and terracotta jacket. Her face
seems full of cheerful longing only;
bright, alone,
she looks to where the rainbow bus will sail,
and having found her, surely miss
the major route, detour fantastically
or fly. At once, the place
seems thronged with open faces; I
magnanimous. Disarmed,

I make a helpless law:
that we, the people, small
bright craft that navigate the malls and squares,
shall not henceforth by any thunderous powers
be caused to founder;
there shall be peace;

the penalty no less
than famous men, imprisoned
in their purposes, shall forfeit
the accidentals of our days,
the given coin of joy.

Buying Tobacco in Spain

She spoke no English, I no Spanish.
A pointless phrase or two, a frown, a shrug.
At last we gave up words and lifted off

in the simple, sumptuous grammar of the sign,
mime not quite worthy of Marceau perhaps,
but a warming intimacy of hands

and meeting eyes. 'O.K.'
was the only word that passed,
and I said, 'Gracias'. But then

it came to money – and suddenly those little
paper tokens with their codes and falderals
and etchings of grand buildings and great men

seemed to come between us. (It was partly
that I fumbled, dropped some, couldn't count.)
Very strange they seemed, stranger than language

(stranger even than breathing
hot smoke of shredded leaves).
It wasn't like that on the planet I'm from.
There, we would exchange, oh, things for things,

or things for promises; or, sometimes,
songs for remedies.

Girl in the Baker's Shop

She wears flat shoes and ankle socks; her hair
is almost captured by a clasp. At fifty-five
I wander by, and glance – not stare -
past autumn loaves and tiny vivid cakes
at her oval, perfect face.
I have seen practised smiles, but this,
repeated as may be, seems formed of grace
and innocence. My life's engaged

with the vast necessity to use
my intellect, or spoiled
with correspondence, or the news;
masked therefore beyond semblance
of wooing, and for bread alone,
I visit her surviving excellence.

To Natalie, at the Check-out

I say thank you every time.
And if you make eye-contact, I say
'Thank you very much'.

Thank you, whose graceful hands
pick up, pick up, pick up,
and let the red eye know.

Thank you for coming here
to do the masquerade, the 'Hi',
as if you knew us all.

To be a moving part, to make
the thing go beep, and with your foot
to make the goods roll on.

'That's lovely', you say, of my
ten-pound notes, and 'Thanks again,
bye-bye'. Yes, au revoir, I'll

see you soon, we'll talk some more,
about my card and am I saving tokens,
and you'll spread another

poly-bag for me, and I shall lay
my lovely money in your palm,
and thank you, thank you very much.

Saying Farewell in Trier

Auf wiedersehen.
One day, may we see
each other once again

– or only one of us see,
the other not looking
or looking inward,

and one or other of us
vaguely recall this face.
Even seeing and not recalling,

even passing and not seeing,
or if never again both anywhere
under the bells of Trier,

may we yet be alive
many years from now.
Auf wiedersehen.

Lightning Source UK Ltd.
Milton Keynes UK
UKOW04f2257090315

247574UK00001B/40/P